Disabilities and Differences

We All Learn

Rebecca Rissman

Heinemann Library
Chicago, Illinois

Customer Service 888-454-2279
Visit our website at www.heinemannlibrary.com

Printed in China by South China Printing Company Limited

13 12 11 10 09
10 9 8 7 6 5 4 3 2 1

Library of Congress Cataloging-in-Publication Data
Rissman, Rebecca.
We all learn / Rebecca Rissman.
p. cm. -- (Disabilities and differences)
Includes bibliographical references and index.
ISBN 978-1-4329-2153-8 (hc) -- ISBN 978-1-4329-2159-0 (pb) 1. Learning--Juvenile literature. I. Title.
LB1060.R57 2009
370.15'23--dc22
                        2008029858

Acknowledgments
The author and publisher are grateful to the following for permission to reproduce photographs: ©agefotostock pp. 9 (It Stock Free), 14 (Banana Stock), 18 (Jeff Greenberg); ©Alamy p. 7 (Janine Wiedel Photolibrary); ©AP Photo pp. 16 (Colin Archer), 23 bottom (Colin Archer); ©Corbis pp. 10 (Ed Kashi), 23 middle (Ed Kashi); ©drr.net pp. 13 (Terry Smith/Mira.com), 15 (Ingo Gotz), 23 top (Ingo Gotz); ©Getty Images pp. 4 (Jack Hollingsworth), 8 (Superstudio), 11 (Mahaux Photography), 19 (Adrian Green), 20 (Ariel Skeelley); ©Heinemann Raintree pp. 17 (Richard Hutchings), 21 (Richard Hutchings); ©PhotoEdit pp. 6 (Elena Rooraid), 22 (Michael Newman); ©Shutterstock p. 12 (Monkey Business Images).

Cover image used with permission of ©zefa (Corbis/Mika). Back cover image reproduced with permission of ©Heinemann Raintree (Richard Hutchings).

Every effort has been made to contact copyright holders of any material reproduced in this book. Any omissions will be rectified in subsequent printings if notice is given to the publisher.

Contents

Differences

We are all different.

Learning

We learn facts.

We learn skills.

We learn to swim.

We learn to read.

How We Learn

People learn in different ways.

People learn in different places.

Some people learn by listening.

Some people learn by seeing.

Some people learn by moving.

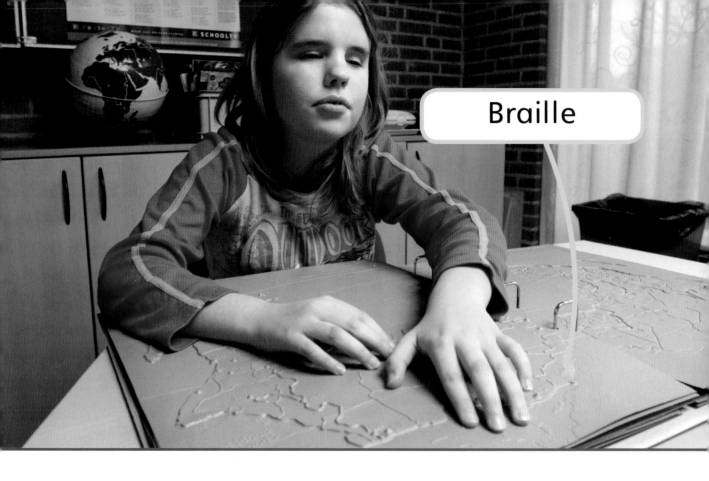

Braille

Some people learn by sitting.

Some people learn by touching.

Some people learn by writing.

Some people learn alone.

Some people learn in groups.

Where We Learn

We can learn at home.

We can learn at school.

We Are All Different

We all learn in different ways.

How do you learn?

Words to Know

 **Braille** raised bumps on paper. People read Braille with their fingers.

 **computer** machine that can help some students communicate, read, and write

 **teacher's aid** person who gives students extra help

This section includes related vocabulary words that can help students learn about this topic. Use these words to explore learning.

Index

Note to Parents and Teachers

Before reading

Ask children to form pairs and find three ways in which they are different, for example height, hair color, eyes, or clothes. Then explain that although they are all unique they also have things in common. Talk to the children about the different ways we learn. Ask them how they think they learn to walk, talk, read, and write. Explain that people learn in different ways and that different skills require different ways of learning.

After reading

Ask the children to work with a partner and to think of three different ways they learn (listening, reading, being shown what to do, or working alone). Collect their answers and make a chart on the board for the students to see. Explain that there are many ways to learn.